Rough Guides

25 Ultimate experiences

India

Make the most of your time on Earth

D0710062

25 YEARS 1982–2007

NEW YORK • LONDON • DELHI

Contents

Introduction

EXPERIENCES have always been at the heart of the Rough Guide concept. A group of us began writing the books **25 years ago** (hence this celebratory mini series) and wanted to share the kind of travels we had been doing ourselves. It seems bizarre to recall that in the early 1980s, travel was very much a minority pursuit. Sure, there was a lot of tourism around, and that was reflected in the guidebooks in print, which traipsed around the established sights with scarcely a backward look at the local population and their life. We wanted to change all that: to put a country or a city's popular culture centre stage, to highlight the clubs where you could hear local music, drink with people you hadn't come on holiday with, watch the local football, join in with the festivals. And of course we wanted to push travel a bit further, inspire readers with the confidence and knowledge to break away from established routes, to find pleasure and excitement in remote islands, or desert routes, or mountain treks, or in street culture.

Twenty-five years on, that thinking seems pretty obvious: we all want to experience something real about a destination, and to seek out travel's **ultimate experiences**. Which is exactly where these **25 books** come in. They are not in any sense a new series of guidebooks. We're happy with the series that we already have in print. Instead, the **25s** are a collection of ideas, enthusiasms and inspirations: a selection of the very best things to see or do – and not just before you die, but now. Each selection is gold dust. That's the brief to our writers: there is no room here for the average, no space fillers. Pick any one of our selections and you will enrich your travelling life.

But first of all, take the time to browse. Grab a half dozen of these books and let the ideas percolate … and then begin making your plans.

Mark Ellingham
Founder & Series Editor, Rough Guides

25

Ultimate
experiences
India

On the frozen river, silence has substance. It's tangible because it means the way ahead is solid, and therefore safe. More than the crack of splintering ice, travellers on this hazardous artery – the only winter route through the Great Himalayan range from the remote region of Zanskar to Ladakh, in the Indus Valley – learn to dread the lap of open water. "This one Tsarak Do . . . 'Running Place'". My guide, Namgyal Tenzing, wrapped in a wine-coloured wool *goncha*, ice dusting his hat and eyelashes, peers upriver through a mist of falling crystals. "Very cold place. Zanskar people is running here. Never stop. No good." This, however, is precisely what I and my three Zanskari companions are about to do.

After eight hours skidding over shattered plate ice, our only chance of shelter turns out to be a rock hollow on the opposite bank. But between us and it, the ice is tinged tell-tale green, and we can all hear the gurgles of a living river beneath our feet.

The crossing, however, turns out to be straightforward, and in no time at all we're huddled around a driftwood fire that spits wild sparks into the night. Later, as we lie wedged together in the cave, I can hear freshly formed ice

01 Chaddar:
The Himalayan
ice highway

fizzing downstream, and the mountains, ghost-like against the star-strewn sky, begin to glow with the first moonlight.

Depending on weather conditions, it can take anywhere between four and ten days – or even longer – to cover the length of the frozen river, which the locals call Chaddar. Given the dangers involved, it's amazing that so many use it to escape their snowbound homeland in midwinter. But for foreigners, the route repays its rigours ten times over. Quite apart from being one of Asia's last true adventures, it offers the chance to experience the inner Himalaya as few outsiders see it: medieval Buddhist monasteries and thatched-roof villages, half-buried under fresh powder snow; frozen waterfalls; herds of ice-encrusted yaks; and monks performing masked *cham* dances – all set against a vast amphitheatre of white peaks.

There are two talismanic words you'll be glad to hear, loud and often, along the way. Stepping gingerly out onto the river the morning after our freezing night in the cave, Namgyal strikes the surface with his stick, scrutinizes the spangle of blue bubbles beneath and calls out *gala dukh!* – "good ice!".

need to know

The frozen river is practicable for around six weeks during January and February. A few trekking agencies in Leh offer it as a package, but bear in mind your usual travel insurance may not cover you.

02 RHYTHM MADNESS AT THE
Thrissur Puram,
Kerala

Kerala is famous for its extravagant festivals, and none is more grand
– or more frenetic – than the annual *Puram* in the central Keralan town
of Thrissur. Caparisoned elephants, ear-shattering drum orchestras,
lavish firework displays and masked dance dramas are common to all
of them, but at Thrissur the scale of proceedings – not to mention the
suffocating pre-monsoon heat – creates an atmosphere that can, to
the uninitiated at least, seem to teeter on the brink of total insanity.

Two rival processions, representing the Tiruvambadi and Paramekkavu
temples, form the focal point. Each lays on a phalanx of fifteen
sumptuously decorated tuskers, ridden by Brahmin priests
carrying silver-handled whisks of yak hair, peacock-feather
fans and bright pink silk parasols. At the centre of
both lines, the elephants' attendants bear golden
images of their temple deity, like soccer players
brandishing a trophy from an open-
top bus victory parade.

Alongside them, ranks of a
hundred or more drummers
mesmerize the crowd with rapid-
fire beats, accompanied by
cymbal crashes and wailing
melodies from players
of the double-
reeded
khuzal.

The *melam* passes through four distinct phases of tempo, each double the pace of the last, with the fastest rhythm of all acting as a cue for those astride the elephants to stand up and brandish their feather fans and hair whisks in coordinated sequences. Meanwhile, the cymbals crash louder, the *khuzals* reach fever pitch and *kompu* trumpets blast away at their loudest and most dissonant.

Just at the point you think things couldn't get any more tumultuous, fireworks explode in the background – to great roars from the crowd. Many people punch the air, some randomly, while others are clearly *talam branthans*, or rhythm "madmen", whose thrusts follow every nuance of the drum patterns. When the fastest speed is played out, the slow march returns and the procession edges forward another few steps before stopping to begin the whole cycle again.

need to know

Puram usually takes place in late May; check with the state tourist office, ⓦwww.keralatourism.org, for exact dates. A dependable hotel, overlooking the maidan where the main procession takes place, is the modern, two-star **Elite International** (ⓦwww.hoteleliteinternational.com); during the festival, room rates start at around Rs1000 (US$22).

03

Bollywood Glitz

at the Mumbai Metro

If you've never seen a Bollywood movie before, think John Travolta and Olivia Newton-John in *Grease*, pump up the colour saturation, quadruple the number of dancing extras, switch the soundtrack to an AR Rahman *masala* mix, and imagine Indo-Western hybrid outfits that grow more extravagant with every change of camera angle.

Like their classic forerunners of the 1970s and 80s, modern Bollywood blockbusters demand the biggest screens and heftiest sound systems on the market, and they don't come bigger or heftier than those in the recently revamped Metro cinema in Mumbai, the *grande dame* of the city's surviving Art Deco picture houses. A palpable aura of old-school glamour still hangs over the place, at its most glittering on red-carpet nights when huge crowds gather in the street outside for a glimpse of stars such as Shah Rukh Kahn or Ashwariya Rai posing for the paparazzi in front of the iconic 1930s facade.

A sense of occasion strikes you the moment you step into the Metro's foyer, with its plush crimson drapery and polished Italian marble floors. The recent refit has transformed the auditorium into a state-of-the-art multiplex, complete with six screens, lashings of chrome and reclining seats, but the developers had the good sense to leave the heritage features in the rest of the building intact. Belgian crystal chandeliers still hang from the ceilings, reflected in herringbone-patterned mirrors on the mid-landing, with original stucco murals lining the staircases.

While the Metro may have had a makeover, the same quirky conventions that have styled Indian cinema for decades still very much hold sway – in spite of Bollywood's glossier modern image and bigger budgets. So while the waistlines have dropped and cleavages become more pronounced, the star-crossed hero and heroine still have to make do with a coy rub of noses rather than a proper kiss.

Down in the stalls of the Metro, meanwhile, the new decor hasn't subdued behaviour in the cheaper seats. Shouting at the screen, cheering every time the hero wallops someone, and singing along with the love songs are still very much part of the *filmi* experience – even if overpriced popcorn has surplanted five-rupee wraps of peanuts.

Mumbai's Metro Cinema stands on Dhobi Talao Junction, at the top of Azad Maidan, a five-minute cab ride from CST (VT) Station. Circle tickets cost Rs100 (US$2) and should be booked in advance – go to ⓦwww.adlabscinemas.com.

4 Eating a
banana-leaf lunch,
Chidambaram

"Step in!", reads the sign, "for: idly-wada-dosai-utthapam-appam-pongal . . . and rice plate!". You might not know what any of the promised gastronomic delights are, but the aromas of freshly cooked spices, smoky mustard oil, simmering coconut milk and sandalwood-scented incense billowing into the street are enticement enough to do just as the sign says.

In the temple towns of Tamil Nadu, where regional cooking styles have been refined over centuries in the kitchens of the great Chola shrines, "meals" or "rice-plate" restaurants are where most working men – and travellers – eat. Some are swankier than others, with air-con instead of paddle fans, but none serve tastier or more traditional south Indian food than Sri Ganesa Bhawan, in the shadow of the famous Nataraja temple in Chidambaram.

For lunch, space in the old-fashioned dining room is always at a premium – you'll probably find yourself squeezing on to a table of pilgrims, hair neatly oiled and caste marks smeared over their foreheads, who'll greet you with a polite wobble of the head. Once seated, a boy in a grubby cotton tunic will unroll a plantain leaf, which you sprinkle water on. This acts as a signal for a legion of other, older boys in less grubby tunics to swing into action, depositing ladles of rice, fiery *rasam* broth and lip-smacking curries on to your glossy green plate.

The various dishes are always consumed in the same set order, but chances are you won't have a clue what this is – much to the amusement of your fellow diners, who will by now be watching you intently. Mixing the various portions together with the rice, yoghurt, buttermilk and sharp lime pickle, and then shovelling them into your mouth with your fingers, requires a knack you won't get the hang of straight away. Not that it matters in the least. Underscored by the tang of tamarind, fried chilli, fenugreek seeds and fresh coconut, the flavours will be surprising, delicious and explosive, regardless of how you combine them.

need to know

Sri Ganesa Bhawan, on West Car St (no phone), serves lunch between 11.30am and 2.30pm; a filling rice-plate here, or at any of the many places like it, will cost around Rs35 (US$0.75). After 2.30pm, a snack menu – dominated by griddle-fried rice- and lentil-flour dosai pancakes – replaces the full-scale rice meal.

Of all India's holy rivers, the Ganges – or "Ganga" as it's known in Sanskrit – is considered by Hindus to be the holiest. And of all the sacred sites along its course, the most sacred is the spot, high in the Garhwal Himalaya, where its waters first see the light of day.

Aside from bringing you much spiritual merit (a mere wind-borne droplet of Ganga water is believed to purge the body of a hundred lifetimes of sin), the pilgrimage to the river's source provides the fastest possible route into the heart of the world's highest mountain range. Winding through rhododendron and deodar cedar forests, a paved road runs nearly all the way from the Indian plains to Gangotri, at an altitude of 3200 metres.

a mere wind-borne droplet of Ganga water is believed to purge the body of a hundred lifetimes of sin

From here on, you have to join the ragged procession of pilgrims and ash-smeared sadhus as they cover the final twenty-kilometre leg: a long day's walk over a moonscape of grey dust and scree. Laden with sacks of offerings and supplies, many chant the 108 honorific titles of the river as they walk: "Imperishable", "A Sun Among the Darkness and Ignorance" or "Cow Which Gives Much Milk". And for once, the earthly splendour of the surroundings still lives up to its mythology.

Having crossed a rise on the valley floor, the full glory of the Gangotri Glacier is suddenly revealed, snaking away to a skyline of smouldering black and white snow peaks. A 400-metre vertical wall, grey-blue and encrusted with stones, forms the awesome snout of the ice floe – Gau Mukh, the "Cow's Mouth". For the community of sadhus who live semi-naked in this freezing spot year-round, nearly 4000 metres above sea level, there's nowhere on earth more uplifting. Come here at dawn, and you'll see them plunging into the icy water surging from the foot of the glacier, wringing it out of their long dreadlocks and settling down on the eroded rocks of the riverbank to meditate or practice yoga.

Even without the magnificent mountain backdrop the source would be one of the most enthralling places on earth. But with the crystal-clear mountain light, the rituals and the vast amphitheatre of rock and ice rising on all sides, the atmosphere is nothing short of transcendental.

Trekking to
the source of the Ganges

need to know

Gangotri is accessible from May until October. Most visitors bed down for the night in a dorm at the state-run Tourist Bungalow, in the village of Bhojbasa, 5km short of the glacier.

We'd known they were on their way since breakfast time, when news that the arribida had formed a couple of kilometres out to sea crackled through our shortwave radio from the spotter ship. First reports suggested that numbers were good. The Indian coastguard had forecast a steady on-shore breeze blowing from the Bay of Bengal until dawn, and the military firing range nearby, forewarned of the invasion, had agreed to suspend artillery tests and cut its lights. After a week of scanning the eastern horizon, the stage was set for one of the world's great wildlife spectacles.

The first olive ridleys reached us around sunset. After their epic swim across half of the planet's oceans, the pregnant females arrive exhausted and silent, allowing the surf to wash them as far up the incline as possible before starting their struggle with the undertow and soft sand. Within half an hour, the beach is entirely covered: a huge undulating sweep of hump-backed shells, glistening under a full moon.

An estimated 240,000 marine turtles crawled on to Gahirmatha beach that night, watched by barely thirty or so people from the Greenpeace Turtle Witness Camp.

By the time they'd laid their batch of eggs, many were too drained to move, submitting with watery-eyed indifference to the attentions of us onlookers. Then, as if in response to some pre-arranged signal, the whole arribida suddenly started lumbering seaward again, leaving behind them an empty beach crisscrossed with myriad prints.

The cool of early morning allowed us a few hours sleep back at camp before we too had to begin our journeys homewards, in the opposite direction: via the crowded cities of coastal Orissa. Bumping along in the back of a local bus, I tried to work out where I'd be in forty days' time when the tiny turtle hatchlings would emerge from their nests and scuttle into the waves to start their long and perilous swim to the Pacific.

06 *The turtle* **ARRIBIDA**, *Orissa*

need to know

The Orissan turtle arribida takes place in late February to March. Precise dates, and details of the Turtle Witness Camp, are obtainable through Greenpeace India (www.greenpeace.org/india).

07 Sunrise over the Achyutaraya Temple, Hampi

When Vijayanagar, capital of India's last Hindu empire, was ransacked by a Muslim army after the Battle of Talikota in 1565, the devastation was total. Few temples, palaces, houses or human lives were spared. It was the sixteenth-century equivalent of a nuclear holocaust.

Today, the site still lies largely deserted and in ruins – save for the mighty Virupaksha Temple at its heart, in the village of Hampi. Ranged around a bend in the Tungabhadra River, the small bazaar village and archeological remains occupy a landscape of surreal beauty. Hills of smooth granite boulders, eroded through time, are separated from each other by swathes of brilliant green banana groves, which conceal colonnaded walkways leading to hidden temples and bathing tanks. Because they were so comprehensively destroyed, the monuments possess an aura of greater antiquity than they perhaps deserve, but this only adds to the charisma of the place.

You can spend days wandering between sites, clambering up flights of rock-cut steps to reach forgotten shrines, deciphering mythological friezes on the walls of collapsed palaces, or catching coracles across the river to visit caves inhabited by dreadlocked sadhus. The definitive Hampi experience, however, has to be watching the sun rise from Matanga Hill, just east of the village's long, straight bazaar. Having scaled the flight of steps leading to the tiny temple crowning its summit, a wondrous view opens up. Immediately below you, the *gopuras* and walled enclosures of the Achyutaraya Temple rise through the morning mist like a vision from a lost world, framed by a vista of boulder hills stretching to the horizon.

And if that weren't a perfect enough way to start your day, an entrepreneurial *chai*-wallah has set up shop on the temple rooftop, so you can enjoy the awesome spectacle over a cup of delicious hot tea.

08
Crowd-watching at Kartik Purnima, Pushkar

In this era of **"Readymade Suitings and Shirtings"**, traditional Indian dress is definitely on the decline. There is, however, one place you're guaranteed to see **proper old-fashioned finery** at its most elaborate and flamboyant. Each year, during the **full-moon phase of Kartika month**, tens of thousands of Rajasthani villagers hitch up their camel carts and converge on the oasis of Pushkar, on the **edge of the Thar desert**, for a bathe in the town's sacred lake, whose waters are said to be especially purifying at this time. As well as a redemptive dip, the festival also provides an opportunity to indulge those other great Rajasthani passions: **trading livestock, arranging marriages – and generally strutting one's stuff.**

Kartik Purnima has in recent times been rebranded as the **Pushkar Camel Fair** by the region's entrepreneurial tourist office. For sure, the vast sea of neatly clipped beige fur undulating in the dunes around the town during the festival presents one of India's most arresting spectacles. But it's the animals' owners **who really steal the show**. Dressed in kilos of **silver jewellery**, flowing pleated skirts and veils dripping

Kartik Purnima is usually held in early November. Check ⓦwww. rajasthantourism.gov.in for the exact dates and details of special tent camps erected around the town to accommodate the tens of thousands of visitors who come for the festival.

with intricate mirrorwork and **embroidery**, the women look **breathtaking against the desert backdrop**, especially in the warmer colours of evening, when the sand glows molten red and the sky turns a fantastic shade of mauve. The men go for a more sober look, but compensate for their **white-cotton dhoti loin cloths and shirts** with outsized, vibrantly coloured turbans and **handle-bar moustaches** waxed to pin-sharp points.

Traditional Rajasthani garb looks even more wonderful against the backdrop of Pushkar's **sacred steps**, or ghats, spread around the lake. For the full effect, get up before dawn, when the **drumming, conch-blowing and bell-ringing** starts at the temples, and position yourself on one of the flat rooftops or **peeling whitewashed cupolas** overlooking the waterside. When the **sun's first rays** finally burst across Nag Pahar ("Snake Mountain") to the east, a **blaze of colour erupts** as thousands of pilgrims gather to invoke **Brahma**, the Supreme Creator Being of Hindu mythology, by raising little brass pots of sacred water above their heads and pouring them back into the lake. It's a **scene that has changed little in hundreds – even thousands – of years.**

The Taj by moonlight

09

When it comes to viewing the Taj Mahal, there isn't really an unflattering angle or wrong kind of weather. Even the Dickensian smog that can roll off the Jamuna River in mid-winter only serves to heighten the mystique of the mausoleum's familiar contours. The monsoon rains and grey skies of August also cast their spell: glistening after a storm, the white marble, subtly carved and inlaid with semi-precious stones and Koranic calligraphy, seems to radiate light.

The world's most beautiful building was originally commissioned by the Mughal emperor Shah Jahan in the 1630s as a memorial to his beloved wife, the legendary beauty Arjumand Bann Begum, or Mumtaz Mahal ("Elect of the Palace"), who died giving birth to their fourteenth child. It is said that Shah Jahan was inconsolable after her death and spent the last years of his life staring wistfully through his cusp-arched window in Agra Fort at her mausoleum downriver.

The love and longing embodied by the Taj are never more palpable than during the full-moon phase of each month, when the Archeological Survey of India opens the complex at night. For once, the streams of visitors flowing through the Persian-style Char Bagh Gardens leading to the tomb are hushed into silence by the building's ethereal form, rising melancholically from the river bank.

Shah Jahan's quadrangular water courses, flanking the approaches, are specially filled for full-moon visits, as they would have been in Mughal times. The reflections of the luminous walls in their mirror-like surfaces seem to positively shimmer with life, like the aura of an Urdu

devotional poem or piece of sublime sitar music. At such moments, it's easy to see why the Bengali mystic-poet, Rabindranath Tagore, likened the Taj Mahal to "... a teardrop on the face of Eternity".

need to know

The Taj Mahal is open from 6am to 7pm daily except Friday. Over the four days of a full moon, you can also visit (in half-hour slots) between 8pm and midnight. Tickets, which cost Rs750 (US$16) for foreigners and Rs20 for Indians, must be booked one day in advance at the hatches at the main entrance.

10 An elephant safari, Kaziranga

Never ride an elephant on an empty stomach. Lolloping along nine feet off the ground atop a bristly pachyderm before breakfast can induce a kind of motion sickness – which is why I happened to be chewing a day-old chapatti when I had my most memorable wildlife encounter ever.

need to know

Kaziranga is located 217km east of the Assamese capital, Guwahati. The park is open from November until April. Elephant rides depart daily between 5am and 7am.

We'd been at Kaziranga, in the northeastern state of Assam, for a couple of days. The monsoon rains had petered out and the Brahmaputra, whose waters completely flood the park for several months each summer, had receded, leaving in their wake an abundance of small lakes, marshes and reedbeds teeming with birds and animals. In the space of half an hour, we'd sighted chital and sambar, nilgai (blue bulls), bison, wild elephant and, before the last wisps of straggling mist had disappeared from the treetops, our first rhino of the day.

Emerging slowly from a stand of elephant grass to our right, she'd stopped, raised a imperious horned nose to the air and ambled blinking into the sunlight, followed by her inquisitive calf and two more adults. Camera shutters whirred as the family group made its way to the banks of a nearby waterhole, by now each with a snowy white egret perched on its back.

Then something amazing happened. Our elephant, Laxmi, started shivering – not from the cold, but with naked fear. The mahout raised a hand, pointing to a break in the grass just next to where the rhinos had first appeared. There, frozen in mid-step, its striped face staring straight up at us, was a huge tiger. Unable to turn tail unnoticed, she instead decided to brazen the moment out and crept with feigned nonchalance in front of us, barely a few metres away.

Seeing tigers and rhinos in such proximity is an experience you'd never be able to have anywhere else. Established for over a century, Kaziranga is one of the world's richest wildlife sanctuaries: around 80 percent of the planet's total Indian rhino population lives within its borders, and the current tiger density is the highest in the country.

Back at the waterhole, the rhinos had got scent of our big cat and ushered their calf away. After a yawn and stretch, the tiger soon slunk off too, leaving us with plenty to savour on our long plod back to breakfast.

The dancing goddess, Kerala

A sudden intensification of the **drumming and cymbal rhythms** heralds the appearance of the Teyyam. The crowd of villagers falls silent. **Bare-chested** and wrapped in white cotton lunghis, the men and boys stand on one side, the women, in **coloured silk saris** with garlands of **jasmine strung in their hair**, stand on the other. Excitement, tempered with apprehension, flickers across their faces, turning in an instant to **wide-eyed awe** as the deity finally emerges from behind the village shrine.

It's hard to convey the **electric mix of terror and adoration** the Teyyam's costume inspires. A huge confection of **gold-painted papier-mâché, metal jewellery, appliqué hangings, cowry-shell anklets and ornate necklaces**, surmounted by a vast corona of **silver foil and crimson fur**, its focal point is an elaborately made-up face with curly chrome fangs protruding from its mouth.

This is as close to the goddess as some of these people will ever get. Age-old caste restrictions still bar them from access to Kerala's most revered Tantric shrines, but at this moment **Muchilôttu Bhagavati**, a local form of the Hindu goddess of death and destruction, **Kali, is herself manifest among them**, her spirit glaring through the Teyyam's bloodshot eyes, animating its every move and gesture.

Twisting and spinning through a succession of poses in the firelight, the apparition **really does feel like a visitor from another realm**. **Temple drumming and chants** accompany her graceful dance around the beaten-earth arena, which grows in intensity through the night, culminating in a **frenzied possession**. Only when the first daylight glows through the palm canopy does the deity retire, blessing her devotees as she does so.

need to know

Teyyattam rituals are held across the north of Kerala from November through March. They're held for all kinds of reasons: to celebrate the safe return of a son from the Gulf, the construction of a new house or as part of a temple feast, and take on an amazing number of forms. The simplest way to find one is to call at the tourist office in Kannur (Cannanore), which can check the local Malayalam newspapers for notices.

Birding by rickshaw, Keoladeo

"Sir-Madam. Indian helicopter for safari?" The joke was an old one we'd heard a hundred times in Agra, but the cycle rickshaw-wallah's English was impeccable. And he certainly seemed to know his birds. "All 220 resident species and 140 migrants I can identify: painted stork, brahminy duck, purple sunbird, laughing thrush, jungle babbler, Indian roller, blue-tailed bee-eater, common drongo ..."
"Ok, ok – let's go!"

As it turned out, our "pilot-cum-guide", Amar Singh, was worth every rupee of his fee. Keoladeo, India's famous bird park on the Rajasthan–Uttar Pradesh border, is largely roadless. But though this former royal hunting reserve spread over 29 square kilometres of misty wetlands is closed to motorized traffic, the dusty tracks that skirt its marshes, lagoons and lakes, edged by acacia and slender tamarind trees, are perfect terrain for bicycles. Moreoever, Amar knew where exactly where the largest congregations of birds were to be found.

Bouncing through early morning fog on the back of a dilapidated Indian cycle rickshaw is a novel way to spot wildlife, and one that's possibly unique to Keoladeo. Elephant-back it isn't, but the trusty Indian helicopter allows you to get really close to the flocks of pelicans, brightly coloured ducks and herons and egrets that paddle through the shallows.

The park is a whirl of movement. Electric-blue kingfishers flash past your nose; paradise flycatchers with exquisite long white tails pull aerobatic stunts directly overhead; and ospreys flap dripping wet out of the water only a few feet away, huge fish writhing in their talons.

Most striking of all, though, are Keoladeo's human-sized Saras cranes, giant blue-grey birds with scarlet heads and yellow beaks that creep in slow motion through the reed beds, usually in pairs, and often barely a stone's throw from the rickshaw. And then there's the constant cacophony on all sides – of birds feeding, nesting, mating, grooming, or just squawking from the tree tops.

The racket eases off as you enter the southern limits of the park, half an hour's pedalling from the main gates. We'd come to this far-flung corner of Keoladeo in search of black buck and sambar deer, and might well have stayed long enough to spot some had Amar not told us a solitary tiger had been sighted here only the week before, hunting at the water's edge. I found myself suddenly wondering how fast a cycle-rickshaw could go at full pelt.

need to know

Keoladeo is open year round, but the best time to visit is between October and March. Cycle rickshaw safaris cost from around Rs75 (US$1.65) per hour and can be arranged on arrival at the park gates.

Rising from the surrounding plains of tropical vegetation like man-made mountains, the great temples of the Chola dynasty utterly dominate most major towns in Tamil Nadu. For sheer scale and intensity, though, none outstrips the one dedicated to the Fish-Eyed Goddess, Shri Meenakshi, and her consort, Sundareshwara, in Madurai. Peaking at 46m, its skyscraping *gopuras* stand as the state's pride and joy – Dravidian India's Empire State, Eiffel Tower and Cristo Redentor rolled into one. The towers taper skywards like elongated, stepped pyramids, every inch of their surfaces writhing with an anarchic jumble of deities, demons, warriors, supernatural beasts, curvaceous maidens, pot-bellied dwarves and sprites – all rendered in Disney-bright colours, and topped with crowns of gigantic cobra heads and gilded finials.

Joining the flood of pilgrims that pours through the gateways beneath them, you leave the trappings of modern India far behind. A labyrinth of interconnecting walkways, ceremonial halls and courtyards forms the heart of the complex. Against its backdrop of 30,000 carved pillars unfolds a never-ending round of rituals and processions. Day and night, cavalcades of bare-chested priests carry torches of burning camphor and offerings for the goddess, accompanied by drummers and musicians blasting out devotional hymns on Tamil oboes. Shaven-headed pilgrims prostrate themselves on the greasy stone floors, as queues of women clutching parcels of lotus flowers, coconuts and incense squeeze through the crush to the innermost sanctum.

Perhaps the most amazing thing of all about the Meenakshi Temple is that these rituals have taken place in the same shrines, continually and largely unchanged, since the time of ancient Greece. Nowhere else in the world has a classical civilization survived into the modern era, and nowhere else in India are the ancient roots of Hinduism so tangible. It's as if Delphi or the Acropolis were still centres of active worship in the dot-com era.

need to know

Madurai, in the south of Tamil Nadu, can be reached by plane from Mumbai (3hr 20min) or the state capital, Chennai (1hr). The Shri Meenakshi-Sundareshwara Temple is open to non-Hindus.

India's Acropolis:

Shri Meenakshi–Sundareshwara Temple, Madurai

13

Peaking at 46m, the towers taper skywards like elongated, stepped pyramids, every inch of their surfaces writhing with an anarchic jumble of deities, demons, warriors, supernatural beasts, curvaceous maidens, pot-bellied dwarves and sprites.

Exploring the Thar Desert by camel, **Jaisalmer**

In defiance of its old Rajasthani name, **Marusthali (Land of Death)** the Thar is the most **densely populated of the world's great deserts**. From the cities on its fringes all the way to the India–Pakistan border, the vast sand flats spreading across the northwest of the subcontinent are dotted with **myriad tiny mud and thatch villages**, most of them many miles from the nearest stretch of tarmac.

A train line and national highway wind in tandem to Jaisalmer, the Thar's most remote and beautiful citadel town, but from there on, the only way to reach the desert's more isolated settlements is by camel.

Riding out into the scrub, six feet off the ground, with the honey-coloured ramparts and temple towers of Jaisalmer fort receding into the distance, you enter another kind of India – one of wide, shimmering vistas, endless blue skies and, when the rolling gait of your camel ceases, profound stillness. The landscape is no great shakes: apart from a few picture-book dunes blistering up here and there, the Thar is monotonously flat.

Rather, it's for the flamboyance of the desert settlements that most visit this stark borderland. Perhaps as compensation for the sandy drabness of their world, the villagers adorn their children, their animals, houses, carts, shrines – and themselves – in elaborate style. Adobe walls are enlivened with elegant ochre and red geometric patterns; kitchen utensils with squiggly green and blue lacquerwork; moulded mud interiors, clothes and furniture with fragments of sparkling mica, cowry shells or embroidery.

Packs of jubilant children scamper out of every village as soon as a line of camels hoves into view. And the same pack follows you out again afterwards, which is perhaps why trekking camps tend to be in the middle of nowhere, well beyond foraging range. At sunset, saddle sore and a little sunburned, you can sit back and reflect on the day's encounters as the desert glows red in the dying light. Sprawled on a rug beside a flickering campfire, with a pan of smoky dal and rice bubbling away under the starriest of skies, the Thar can feel a lot less like a "Land of Death" than a wholesome, blissful retreat.

need to know

Camel treks lasting from one day to fourteen, or more, can be arranged through any Jaisalmer hotel or tourist office for Rs400–1500 (US$8.80–33) per night, depending on the level of comfort. The cool winter months, between early December and the end of January, are the best times to go.

15

The sun had barely risen above the riverbanks, but already the cremation ghats were hard at work. Four corpses, tightly bound in cotton and still soaked from their final cleansing dip in the Ganges, were laid out on wood pyres, ghee and garlands of orange marigolds piled on top of them. While gangs of small, dark, muscular men fed the flames, grieving relatives looked on, murmuring prayers with palms pressed together and heads bowed. The surrounding buildings were black with soot.

CITY OF LIGHT:
Boating down the Ganges at Varanasi

Varanasi – or Kashi ("City of Light"), as it was known in ancient times – is Hinduism's holiest city. Infamous across India for its squalor, its old core is a teeming, warrenous tangle of narrow alleyways with intricately carved doorways opening on to hidden, high-walled courtyards and shrines. Wander around for long enough and you'll eventually emerge at the ghats, or sacred stone steps, which spread around the mighty bend in the river here. From dawn until dusk, they present a constantly animated canvas of bathers, sadhus, tourists, hawkers, stray cows and priests plying their age-old trade under ragged parasols – all set against a magnificent backdrop of crumbling temples and palaces.

The best way to enjoy the spectacle is to jump in a rowing boat at Asi Ghat, in the south of the old city, just before sunrise. Paddling north as the first rays of daylight infuse the riverfront with a reddish glow, you glide past the dark stupas of Buddha Ghat, Rewa Ghat's distinctive leaning towers, and the candy-striped steps of Vijayanagar Ghat. Manikarnika, the cremation ghat, is where the boatmen generally turn around.

Out on the river, visitors are insulated from the hassle of guides and trinket sellers, but not necessarily from Varanasi's still less savoury aspects. Poor Hindus who can't afford enough wood for their pyres will often have their charred remains shoved unceremoniously into the water – it's not unusual to find your boat bumping into a bloated body part, or even something eating one.

The ghats themselves are, however, most atmospheric just before dark. Watching the priests' cane lanterns flickering to life and mingling with the reflections of the afterglow, Kashi feels every inch the mystical "Threshold of Eternity" it has always been for Hindus.

need to know
Boat rides cost anything between Rs100 and Rs500 (US$2.20–11.20), depending on demand and your ability to haggle.

A walk to "Paradise", Gokarna

Goa tends to be where most people head when they fancy a beach break. There is, however, one special little town a couple of hours further south down the coast, where you can hit the sands without feeling like you've left India entirely behind.

As the site of one of the country's most revered Shiva shrines, Gokarna has been an important Hindu pilgrimage destination for thousands of years. Like a lot of India's religious centres, it's locked in a charismatic time warp: worn and dilapidated, but full of old-world atmosphere. Brahmin priests still saunter around bare-chested, swathed in white or coral-coloured lunghis, and the main market street is always thronged with stray cows and bus loads of pilgrims squelching their way from the town's sacred beach to the temples after a purifying dip in the sea.

A lone Rama temple, overlooking Gokarna's seafront from the edge of a headland wrapped in waxy green cashew bushes, marks the start of a path to an altogether different kind of beach scene. Backed by coconut groves and forested hills, the series of beautiful bays to the south is where the hardcore hippy contingent forced out of Goa by the 1990s charter boom re-grouped and put down roots.

Of all of them, Om Beach, where a pair of twin coves and their rocky outcrops replicate the sacred Hindu symbol for "Oneness and Peace", is the most famous. Further south, the path continues beyond steep, grassy clifftops dotted with miniature palms and red laterite boulders to a string of even more gorgeous side coves with names like "Full-Moon" and "Paradise". This far away from civilization, the jungle descends right to the sand line, while the sea crashes in wild and clean. Fish eagles patrol the foreshore and dolphins regularly flip out of the waves.

Admittedly, the kind of ersatz Indian behaviour beloved in these hideaways isn't for everybody. But if the ostentatious chillum-smoking, yoga posing and mantra-chanting does start to grate, rest assured you can always slip one of the local fishermen a fifty-rupee note and have him whisk you back to town to watch the real thing.

need to know

Gokarna is most easily accessible
via the Konkan Railway, which
connects Mumbai with Kerala. Hotels
and guest houses provide plenty of
accommodation in town, but you can
also sleep on the beaches in locally run
thatch and bamboo huts.

17

The journey over the roof of the world: the Manali–Leh Highway

"Unbelievable is it Not!" reads a road sign at Tanglang La – at 5360m the highest point on the Manali–Leh highway. Looking north from the thicket of prayer flags fluttering above the pass, you'll probably find yourself agreeing. Between you and the white line of the Karakorams in the distance stretches a vast, bone-dry wilderness of mountains and snow-dusted valleys – not a view you'd normally expect from a bus window.

The 485-kilometre route from Manali in Himachal Pradesh to Leh in Ladakh is the great epic among Indian road journeys. With an overnight stop at altitude under a makeshift parachute tent en route, it takes two days to cover, carrying you from the foothills of the Himalayas to the margins of the Tibetan Plateau. Weather conditions can be fickle – blizzards descend even in mid-summer – and facilities along the way are rough and ready, to say the least. But the privations pale into insignificance against the astonishing scenery.

The first, and most formidable, of the obstacles to be crossed is Rohtang La, "Pile of Bones Pass". Straddling one of the most sudden and extreme climatic transitions on the planet, Rohtang overlooks lush green cedar woods and alpine meadows on one side, and on the other a forbidding wall of chocolate- and sand-coloured scree, capped by ice peaks trailing plumes of spindrift.

Once across, settlements are few and far between. Nomadic shepherds and their flocks are sometimes the only signs of life on gigantic mountainsides streaked purple, red and blue with mineral deposits. Packed under snow for most of the year, the road surface deteriorates as you gain altitude, crumbling to loose shale and dizzying voids.

You cross Tanglang La late on the second afternoon, reaching the first Ladakhi villages soon after. Swathed in kidney-shaped terraces of ripening barley, each is surveyed by its own fairy-tale Buddhist monastery, with golden finials gleaming from the rooftops in sunlight of an almost unearthly clarity.

need to know The Manali–Leh Highway is officially open between June 21 and September 15, although buses tend to run as long as the passes remain free of snow. You can also tackle it by mountain bike, which takes around three weeks. Alternatively, you can fly from Delhi to Leh in little more than hour.

Kerala's Kuttinad backwaters region is, in every sense, a world apart from the mainstream of Indian life. Sandwiched between the Arabian Sea and the foothills of the Western Ghat Mountains, its heart is a tangled labyrinth of rivers, rivulets and shimmering lagoons, enfolded by a curtain of dense tropical foliage. This natural barrier screens Kuttinad from the roads, railways and market towns that dominate the rest of the coastal strip, making it blissfully tranquil for such a densely populated area.

Innumerable small vessels glide around Kuttinad, but easily the most romantic way to explore it is in a *kettuvallam*, or traditional Keralan rice barge. Hand-built from teak and jackwood and sporting canopies made from plaited palm leaves, they're beautiful craft – whether propelled along gondolier-style using long poles or by less environmentally friendly diesel engines.

Views constantly change as you cruise along. One minute you're squeezing through a narrow canal clogged with purple water hyacinth; the next, you're gliding over luminous, placid lakes fringed by groves of coconut palms. Every now and then, a whitewashed church tower, minaret or temple finial will reveal the presence of a hidden village. Some settlements occupy only the tiniest parcel of land, barely large enough for a small house. Others have their own vegetable gardens and ranks of cantilevered Chinese fishing nets dangling from the river bank.

18
CRUISING THE
KERALAN
BACKWATERS

Dozens of *kettuvallam* cruise firms compete for custom in towns such as Alappuzha and Karunnagapalli, some offering top-of-the-range rice barges complete with designer cane furniture, gourmet kitchens and viewing platforms scattered with cushions and lanterns. Alternatively, you could eschew such luxury in favour of a more authentic mode of transport: one of the stalwart municipal ferries that chug between Kuttinad's major towns and villages. Aside from saving you the equivalent of the average annual wage of most of your fellow passengers, arriving in one of these oily beasts won't provoke the frenzied response from local kids that can shatter the very tranquility that makes Kuttinad so special.

need to know

Kettuvallam cruises can be arranged through most upscale hotels. Expect to pay anywhere between Rs4000 (US$90) and Rs10,000 (US$220) for a 24-hour cruise, depending on how swish the boat is. Ferries cost just a few rupees.

Even now, with the approach road marred by postcard stalls and car parks, the Ajanta Caves in northern Maharashtra have about them the aura of a lost world. Hollowed out of the sides of a horseshoe-shaped ravine, deep in an arid wilderness zone that has always been forbiddingly remote, the complex remains hidden from view until you're almost directly beneath it. When Lt Alexander Cunningham of the 16th Bengal Lancers stumbled on the site by chance during a tiger hunt in 1813, the excavations had lain forgotten for more than a thousand years – their floors a midden of animal bones and ash from aboriginal hunting fires, their exquisite frescoes blackened by soot.

These days, the worn, rock-cut steps to the caves are fitted with metal handrails, and electricity has replaced the candles used by Cunningham's party, but from the instant the guide first swings his arc light over the murals adorning the walls you're plunged into another time. It's a moment few visitors forget. Once your eyes have adjusted to the swirls of earthy red, yellow, blue and black pigments, scenes of unimaginable sophistication emerge from the gloom: sumptuous royal processions; elaborate court and street scenes; snow-capped mountains; sages; musicians; stormy seascapes and shipwrecks; marching armies; and a veritable menagerie of animals, both real and imagined.

Visions of a
lost civilization,
Ajanta
19

But it's the intimacy of the art that really captivates. The beautifully fluid tableaux seem to glow with life. Kohl-rimmed eyes light up; the well-toned torsos, draped with jewellery, still look sexy; dance poses ooze sensuous grace, humour and vitality; and you can almost smell the aroma of a lotus blossom being raised by the smiling Bodhisattva Avalokitesvara in Cave 1 – India's own Mona Lisa.

For the pilgrims who would have filed past these sacred treasures thousands of years ago, the art would have fired the imagination with a power equivalent to that of modern cinema. These must have been the Bollywood movies of their era, complete with resplendently bejewelled heroines and strong, compassionate heroes, backed up by a supporting cast of thousands – and if the images are anything to go by, the soundtrack would have been amazing.

need to know

The Ajanta Caves are open daily 9am–5.30pm; entrance for foreigners costs US$5. There's little decent accommodation at the site, and most visitors base themselves in the city of Aurangabad, 108km southwest, travelling up by bus or jeep taxi.

There had been an unseasonal downpour and the jungle was literally steaming. Slicks of red mud had spilled over the road in places, repeatedly forcing the bus into first gear. Every time it slowed I noticed the policemen riding shotgun at opposite ends of the vehicle un-shoulder their Enfield rifles and study the forest like hawks. Through the 1990s, the Andaman Trunk Road, which links the largest islands in this remote archipelago 1000km off the east coast of India, was repeatedly attacked by Jarawa aboriginal people, angry at encroachments on their territory by settlers and loggers. Arrows and spears had rained through bus windows; travellers had been killed and maimed.

Since then, relations between the Jarawa and the mostly Tamil incomers from the mainland had calmed down, but the two still kept their distance. Waiting at a ferry jetty, my fellow passengers fell into stony silence as three Jarawa men paddled out of the mangroves in a dugout. More African- than Asian-looking, they all wore bands of frayed cotton around their heads. Not a glance, let alone a greeting, was exchanged.

The far north of the Andamans has about it the air of a frontier zone. Infrastructure of any kind is minimal, and accommodation basic. The beaches, however, are out of this world. Permits restrict which islands you're supposed to visit, but local fisherman are happy to take you out in boats to little islets not patrolled by the coast guard, where you can camp wild on shell-white sand beside turquoise bays fringed with coral reefs.

Smith Island is one of the most exquisite. A twenty-minute crossing from the tiny port of Arial Bay, it was uninhabited last time I was there, save for a small colony of deeply tanned Westerners living out an Alex Garland fantasy on a remote sandbar. The talk was all of wild elephants, secret springs and the wonders visible off the reef: marine turtles, dugongs and giant manta rays that swooped out of the blue depths like spectres.

After a couple of nights grilling fish over driftwood fires, I began to understand why most had thrown away their permits and decided to stay until the rains came. In fact, it wouldn't surprise me if some were still there, paddling around Jarawa style.

20

On the **edge** in the **Andamans**

47

The shrine, or Dargah, of the Sufi mystic Nizzam-
uddin Auliya, India's most revered Muslim saint, is one among many ancient
vestiges rising from the modern sprawl of south Delhi. Sandwiched incongruously
between a six-lane flyover and a faceless concrete suburb, it stands at the centre of
a warren of narrow alleyways, mosques, onion-domed tombs and shanty huts. To
step into this medieval enclave is to enter a kind of parallel reality where little has
changed since Nizzamuddin's burial here in 1325.

From all over the city, large crowds descend on the Dargah on Thursday evenings to
worship at the saint's candle-lit mausoleum. Rubbing shoulders with the devotees
are always a collection of Sufi ascetics, or pir zadas, dervishes, henna-bearded
Islamic scholars, and priests, who rock back and forth over worn copies of
the Koran, murmuring prayers, chatting or fanning **braziers of**
incense.

A sudden drum roll announces the start of the evening's Qawwali
performance. As many as a dozen qawwals may be lined up, sitting cross-
legged before the entrance to the tomb in long Peshwari frockcoats and
lamb's-wool hats. A couple play harmonium, one will play tabla; the rest
provide clapping percussion and chorus, taking it in turns to sing lead.
The qawwals' job is to inspire hal – spiritual ecstasy – among the
worshippers. They do **this by singing songs** of devotion
to Nizzamuddin, to God and the Prophet; songs whose rhythms and melodies
have the power to move even those who may not understand a single word of
their poetry. As the music gradually picks up pace and volume, the crowd
becomes more and more moved by its hypnotic beats. Hands rise into the
air, heads turn towards the darkening sky and, if the hal is upon them,
dervishes slip into trances and start to
spin or convulse, possessed by adoration of the saint. Such gatherings
can last all night, breaking up only at dawn after one final, tumultuous
cadence.

It's a testament to the spirit of tolerance at the heart of
Sufism that among the worshippers at Nizzamuddin's tomb are invariably
members of all Delhi's faith communities: Sikhs, Hindus and Buddhists, as well as
Muslims. In this age of religious fundamentalism, the unifying power
of Qawwali is more **in demand than ever**.

21 Sufi grooves:
Qawwali at Nizzamuddin, Delhi

need to know

Nizzamuddin lies 6km south of Connaught Circus along the Mathura Road, accessible by bus or, more quickly, by auto-rickshaw. All visitors to the shrine must wear long sleeves, full-length trousers or skirts and something covering the head.

need to know

Bhuj, the capital of Kutch, is accessible by direct overnight train services from Ahmedabad. Guides and transport for trips out to the craft villages north of town are best arranged with the tourist officer in Bhuj's Aina Mahal Museum.

22 Christmas shopping in Kutch

It had taken me an hour of skidding around sandy lanes, in the humid late-November heat, to find the place. Road signs are nonexistent in Kutch, and addresses vague, yet everyone seems to know exactly where you're headed, waving you in the right direction even before you've had time to stop your bike and ask.

I needn't have had any misgivings about turning up uninvited at the house of a renowned lacquerworker – they seemed to be expecting me. "Sit, sit," said a smiling granddaughter, spreading a mat on the beaten-earth floor next to the maestro. Glasses of hot *chai* appeared, along with a carved wooden spoon which the old man, his head wrapped in a huge white turban, started to spin on a lathe he manipulated with his toes. As its handle whirred, bands of brightly dyed wax were applied from zinc crayons, then deftly mixed into swirling patterns. "Fifty rupees!" announced the granddaughter when the wax had cooled. I didn't seem to have much choice in the matter, but considered the spoon a bargain anyway.

Kutch, a pan-shaped island off the northwest coast of Gujarat, is scattered with countless tiny craft villages – a legacy of the local ruling family's welcoming refugee policy. Over the centuries, castes and tribal minorities fleeing persecution were permitted to settle here, bringing with them a wealth of arts and craft traditions.

I rode north next to visit a Harijan ("Untouchable") village famed for its embroidery. A gaggle of young girls, sumptuously attired in rainbow-woven bodices and silver neck rings, greeted me at the edge of their compound. Prompted by their shyer older sisters and mothers, they unfurled rolls of multicoloured stitchwork, sparkling with tiny mirrors. Later, they took me to a neighbouring Muslim village, where I watched a master block-printer make some of the most gorgeous textiles I'd ever seen, and finished up buying copper bells from a blind music teacher.

Buying work direct from the producers is a great way to really get under the surface exoticism of life in this remote corner of India. What's more, Kutchi craft villages offer a stimulating alternative to Christmas shopping at the mall – the lacquered spoon was a big hit with the in-laws.

AT FIRST I THOUGHT it was a severed head, smeared with cow dung ash and sandalwood paste. But then its eyelids fluttered open. A murmur of amazement rippled through the crowd of onlookers. Buried up to his neck, dreadlocks coiled into a luxurious top-knot, the sadhu then began to chant. Around him, smoke curled from a ring of smouldering camphor lamps, fed periodically by a couple of saffron-clad acolytes whose task it was to hassle the crowd for baksheesh.

"How many days is Baba-ji sitting in this way?" I asked one of them. "Eight years, more than", came the reply.

You see many extraordinary things at the Maha Kumbh Mela, India's largest religious festival, held once every twelve years around the confluence of the Ganges, Jamuna and (mythical) Saraswati Rivers near Allahabad. But the penances performed by these wandering Hindu holy men are the ones that make you wince the most.

Standing on one leg or holding an arm in the air until it withers are two popular self-inflicted tortures. Sticking skewers though the genitals or dangling heavy bricks from the penis are others. Most sadhus who gather at the Kumbh, however, gain celestial merit in less ostentatious ways. For them, the simple act of bathing at the confluence during the festival is the fastest possible track to liberation from the cycle of rebirth.

The monastic orders, or *Akharas*, to which they belong erect elaborate tented camps ahead of the big days. Watching each process to the river banks in turn, led by their respective pontiffs enshrined on gilded palanquins and caparisoned elephants, is the great spectacle of the Allahabad Kumbh. Stark naked, their bodies rubbed with ash and vermillion, the lines of dreadlocked sadhus march military-style through the early morning mist, brandishing maces, spears, swords, tridents and other traditional weaponry associated with their *Akhara*.

When they finally reach the waterside, the shivering ranks break into an all-out sprint for the shallows, ecstatically shouting invocations to the Hindu gods, Shiva and Rama. Arguments over pecking order often erupt between rival *Akharas*, and those traditional weapons are sometimes put to traditional uses, turning the foreshore into a bloodbath. Onlookers should avoid getting too close.

Kumbh Mela

need to know

The last Kumbh Mela to take place
at the sacred confluence near
Allahabad was in January 2007. In
2010 the honour will be enjoyed
by the town of Haridwar, 214km
northeast of Delhi.

The gates of the Sikhs' holiest shrine, the Golden Temple in Amritsar, are open to all. Given the desecrations inflicted on the complex by the Indian army in 1984 and 1987, this is an extraordinary fact, and vivid testament to the spirit of inclusiveness and equality at the heart of Sikhism.

Originating in the sixteenth century, the youngest of India's three great faiths drew its converts mainly from the oppressed and disenchanted underclasses of Islam and Hinduism. Philosophically and stylistically, it's very much an amalgam of the two, and nowhere is this hybridity more apparent than in the architecture of the shrine that forms the nerve centre of the temple.

Seemingly afloat on a serene, rectangular lake, the temple's centrepiece, the Harmandir, is adorned with a quintessentially Sikh fusion of Mughal-style domes and Hindu lotus motifs. Smothered in gold leaf, it looks at its most resplendent shortly after dawn, when sunlight begins to illuminate its gilded surfaces and the reflections in the lake shimmer to sublime effect. Before approaching it pilgrims are supposed to bathe and then perform a ritual *parikrama*, or circumambulation of the gleaming

need to know

Amritsar is a six-hour train ride from New Delhi. Both the Golden Temple and Guru-ka-Langar are open 24 hours. Although meals are served free of charge, small donations are welcomed.

marble walkway surrounding the lake. En route, returning Sikh expats in sneakers and jeans rub shoulders with more orthodox pilgrims wearing full-length *shalwar*-camises, beehive turbans and an armoury of traditional sabres, daggers and spears. Despite the weaponry on display, the atmosphere is relaxed and welcoming, even dreamy at times, especially when the temple musician-priests are singing verses from the *Adi Granth*, Sikhism's holy text, accompanied by tabla and harmonium.

Perhaps the most memorable expression of the temple's open-hearted spirit, though, is the tradition of offering free meals at the Guru-ka-Langar, a giant communal canteen next to the temple entrance. Foreign tourists are welcome to join the ranks of Sikh pilgrims and the needy from neighbouring districts who file in and sit together cross-legged on long coir floormats. After grace has been sung, the massive job of dishing up thousands of chapatis and buckets of spicy, black-lentil dal begins. By the time all the tin trays have been collected up and the floors swept for the next sitting, another crowd will have gathered at the gates for the cycle to begin again.

Indians take their cricket very seriously. Bollywood may tug the nation's heart strings, but the exploits of the national cricket team quickens its pulse – often to an unnerving degree. Whole cities grind to a halt for the culmination of test matches; and wars have nearly broken out after tussles with arch-rival Pakistan.

Cricket mayhem
at **Eden Gardens,** Kolkata

And if cricket is India's game, then Kolkata's Eden Gardens is its most hallowed ground. Attending a test or one-day international in the massive stadium – the oldest and biggest in the country – can feel like going to watch a gladiatorial combat at the Coliseum and cup final at the Bernabéu rolled into one. The crowds are vast, nudging 100,000 at capacity, and they're more voluble than any other in the world, unleashing deafening roars and fusillades of firecrackers every time their team takes to the field.

Stepping into such a cauldron for the first time can be an intimidating experience for foreign fans. But once on the terraces the atmosphere turns out to be a lot more welcoming than you'd expect. Kolkatans seem delighted and flattered that you've travelled all the way to the Eden Gardens for what, by the law of averages, will probably be a sound drubbing for your team.

need to know Tickets for the best seats at big games cost around Rs1500 (US$32). Unless you've a local contact, expect to queue for them days in advance.

Watching the last day of the second test against Australia in 2001, the locals in the stands around us spent as much time plying us with food from their tiffin tins as cheering their side on. To our shame, they knew our bowlers' and batsmen's stats better than we did, and even pressed handfuls of firecrackers into our hands for the rare occasions when one of their own wickets fell.

As it turned out, we had little to celebrate that day. India pulled off one the most dramatic comebacks in cricket history to steal the match, and left the field to a tumult that, even by the standards of Eden Gardens, was exceptional. As the final wicket was taken, tens of thousands of flares, firework rockets, drums, trumpets and air-horns unleashed an ear-splitting racket into clouds of sulphurous smoke and beer spray. At once terrifying and hilarious, it was anarchy on a scale that would have left the grandees at Lord's apoplectic.

As one resplendently mustachioed gentleman next to me shouted, "Mister, you are thinking 'this is just not cricket!'"

25

Ultimate
experiences
India
miscellany

1 A population explosion

India's population currently stands at around 1.1 billion. The figure has risen by 20 percent every decade since the 1950s, and India is projected to take over from China as the world's most populous country by 2040.

2 Five great places to stay

Taj Mahal Palace and Tower, Mumbai. India's most grandiloquent colonial hotel.

Umaid Bhavan, Jodhpur. Gigantic royal palace with fabulous Art Deco interiors.

Lake Palace Hotel, Udaipur. A Rajput fantasy of domes and cusped arches, seemingly afloat on Lake Pichola.

Bangaram Island Resort, Lakshadweep. Exclusive eco-resort on a tiny coral atoll, 400km off the coast of Kerala.

Imperial Hotel, New Delhi. Stately Raj-era style hotel, in the heart of the capital.

3 Betelmania

Wherever you go in India you'll see people spitting long squirts of expectorated **betel juice** on to pavements, street corners and walls. The ubiquitous crimson spittle is a by-product of the country's number one bad habit: chewing *paan*, a preparation based on areca nut and intensified with tobacco and lime paste. At any given time, hundreds of millions of Indians may be under its mildly narcotic influence.

 Religion

More than 82 percent of India's population follows **Hinduism** – less an orthodox faith than an amalgam of disparate religious rituals and practices dating back four or five millennia. Islam came to India, via Afghanistan and Central Asia, in the tenth and eleventh centuries and is the now the religion of 12 percent of Indians. The rest of the population comprises Sikhs, Jains, Buddhists and Christians.

"Man is made by his beliefs. As he believes, so he is."

Bhagavad Gita

▶▶ Top five religious sites

Golden Temple, Amritsar. Holiest shrine of the Sikhs.

Khwaja Muin-uddin Chishti Dargah, Ajmer. Seven visits to the tomb of this Sufi saint are held to be equal to one to Mecca.

Shree Meenakshi-Sundareshwara Temple, Madurai. The mother of all South Indian temples.

Sabarimala Forest shrine to the God Ayappa, deep in the Western Ghat mountains, which receives 1.5 million devotees during the festival of Makara Sankranti each December and January.

Varanasi Every Hindu hopes to make at least one pilgrimage to India's most sacred city, on the banks of the Ganges, and to have their ashes scattered there after cremation.

5 The national brew

Although tea has been drunk in China for thousands of years, it wasn't grown commercially in India until the British established plantations in Assam and Darjeeling in the 1830s. Since then, **chai** has become India's national drink, consumed with heaps of milk and sugar, and sometimes a hint of ginger and cardamom.

 # 6 Ayurveda

Ayurveda, literally "Science of Life", is a four-thousand-year-old holistic healing system still widely practised in India. It recognizes three constitutional types: **Vatta** (wind); **Pitta** (heat); and **Kapha** (earth and water). Disease is regarded as an imbalance between these three elements, so it's the imbalance rather than some infection that's treated, using a mixture of herbal remedies, massage, dietetics and lifestyle counselling.

"The butterfly counts not months but moments, and has time enough."

Rabindranath Tagore

 # 7 Film

▶▶ Five Bollywood classics

Pather Panchali ("Song of the Long Road"; 1955). Bengali director Satyajit Ray's 1955 debut, often dubbed "the greatest Indian film ever made".

Mother India (1957) Bollywood classic whose lead actors, Nargis and Sunil Dutt, caused a scandal by later marrying – Sunil had played Nargis's son in the film.

Sholay (1975) This spaghetti western-inspired flick was the most successful Bollywood movie of all time, starring the legendary "Big B" himself, Amitabh Bachchan.

Monsoon Wedding (2001) Mira Nair's witty depiction of a swanky Punjabi wedding in Delhi.

Devdas (2002) The highest grossing Bollywood blockbuster of the past decade, featuring megastars Aishwarya Rai, Shahrukh Khan and Madhuri Dixit.

 8 Border conflict

Since Partition in 1947, India has become embroiled in four major military confrontations with neighbour Pakistan, in addition to dozens of minor skirmishes. The conflict is fuelled by ongoing border disputes over Kashmir. In 2001, the two nuclear powers seemed on the verge of all-out war after Muslim extremists, allegedly armed by Pakistan, stormed the Indian parliament building. An estimated one million men at arms were involved in the ensuing standoff.

> *"It is the habit of every aggressor nation to claim that it is acting on the defensive."*
>
> **Jawaharlal Nehru**

9 Blood on the tracks

India's rail network comprises 42,000 miles (over 60,000km) of track and 14,000 trains, which daily transport around 12 million passengers. It's by far the most dangerous train system on the planet, with four to five hundred crashes annually. Travelling by rail, however, is much safer than using India's buses: 85,000 people die each year on the country's roads.

 10 Dance

Classical Indian dance was originally performed in the context of temple rituals, but by the start of the modern era many regional styles had disappeared altogether. Using ancient stone sculpture and palm-leaf manuscripts, twentieth-century dance gurus from Orissa and Tamil Nadu were able to resurrect forms such as *Odissi* and *Bharatiya Natyam*.

 Food

Each region of India has its own cuisine, distinguished by particular staples, cooking methods and blends of spices. In the south, food tends to be predominantly vegetarian, using less oil, lots of fresh coconut and souring agents such as tamarind paste. In the north, centuries of Muslim influence have given rise to elaborate meat preparations steeped in richer, creamier sauces, which tend to be mopped up with Persian-style naan breads or wheat-flour chapattis.

▶▶ Five Indian dishes to die for...

- **Biryani**: tender lamb slow-baked in spicy saffron rice – a speciality of Hyderabad
- **Paturi maach**: steamed Bengali *bekti* fish in mustard and green chilli sauce
- **Malai kofta**: cheese and potato dumplings served in a creamy lentil gravy – a typical north Indian Mughlai favourite
- **Pepper-garlic crab**: mouthwatering Konkan seafood speciality
- **Masala dosa**: rice- and lentil-flour pancake with a tangy potato filling, originally from the temple town of Udipi, Karnataka

...and where to try them

- **Dum Pukht**, Hyderabad: old recipes from the tables of the Nizams, including legendary biryanis
- **Sonargaon**, Kolkata: top-notch Bengali home cooking on silver platters
- **Bukhara**, New Delhi: often voted the world's best tandoori restaurant
- **Konkan Café**, Mumbai: amazing flavours from the southwest coast
- **Saravana Bhavan**, Chennai: definitive southern cuisine

12 India's greatest empires

Mauryas 320–200 BC
Guptas 300–500 AD
Harshas 500–700 AD
Cholas 846–1216 AD
Delhi Sultanate 1290–1320
Vijayanagar 1336–1565
Mughals 1525–1707
Marathas 1650–1750
British 1750–1947

The richest and most powerful dynasty ever to rule India were the Mughals, descendents of Timur the Great (Tamarlane) from Central Asia. Their empire began with Babur's victory over the Delhi Sultan, Ibrahim Lodi, in 1525, and lasted until the death of Aurangzeb in 1707, after which Mughal power gradually ebbed away to the British. Although nominally Muslims, successive emperors took Hindu brides and drew heavily on indigenous traditions to develop their own arts, architecture, crafts, music, dance and literary traditions. The Mughal legacy is still discernible everywhere in India, from bridal outfits to Bollywood movies.

European influence in India went hand in hand with trade. Since the time of the ancient Greeks, pepper had been shipped to the Mediterranean via the ports of Malabar (modern day northern Kerala). But the commerce exploded after Vasco da Gama's discovery of a maritime route to India in 1510. Military backup of this "peaceful trade", which exported textiles alongside spices, mushroomed into wars of conquest as the rival French, Dutch and British vied with each other to gain control of the supply lines inland, and onward sea lanes to Europe.

"The man who ties his turban in haste, watches it unravel at leisure."

Indian proverb

13 The printed word

▶▶ Books on India

John Keay, *Into India* (1999). The best all-round primer for any first-time visitor.

William Dalrymple, *City of Djinns* (1993). The Indian capital's multi-layered history, uncovered with great relish, wit and erudition by its most acclaimed chronicler.

VS Naipaul, *A Million Mutinies Now* (1990). A beautifully crafted mosaic of different lives from around the country.

Suketu Mehta, *Maximum City: Bombay Lost and Found* (2004). A compelling study of India's biggest, most corrupt and glamorous city.

John Keay, *India Discovered* (2001). The story of how British enthusiasts unlocked the mysteries of India's lost civilizations.

▶▶ Indian fiction

Salman Rushdie, *Midnight's Children* (1980). The story of a man born at the very moment of Independence, whose life mirrors that of modern India itself. It won for Rushdie the Booker of Bookers in 1993.

Vikram Seth, *A Suitable Boy* (1993). A virtuoso novel, anatomizing north Indian society in the Nehru era through a mother's search for an appropriate match for her daughter.

Rohinton Mistry, *A Fine Balance* (1996). Long-time Canadian resident Mistry mines the 1970s Bombay of his childhood for this, his finest novel.

Arundhati Roy, *The God of Small Things* (1997). Booker Prize winner about a well-to-do Keralan family caught up in the snobberies of high-caste tradition.

RK Narayan, *A Malgudi Omnibus* (1994). Three of India's best-loved short novels, set in the imaginary south Indian town of Malgudi.

"An eye for an eye makes us all blind."

Mohandas K Gandhi

 14 Technology

India is the world's second largest producer of computer software after the US. There are 51 million Internet users nationwide, which represents 5 percent of the population.

Around 112.2 million people own mobile phones.

"India is not an underdeveloped country, but rather . . . . a highly developed one in an advanced state of decay."
Shashi Tharoor, *The Great Indian Novel*

15 Cricket crazy

India is mad about cricket, and no other sport gets much of a look in – which goes some way to explaining the country's dismal performance at the 2004 Athens Olympics (one silver medal). Batting legend Sachin Tendulkar, from Mumbai, currently holds the world record for test and one-day international centuries.

16 Number crunching

200 million: the estimated number of cows in India.

550 million: the number of farmers in India.

2 million kg: daily tea production in Assam in high picking season.

15,000: the number of guests at former Tamil Nadu Chief Minister Jayalalitha's son's wedding.

Rs3000: monthly salary of a government-employed monkey-catcher in Delhi.

17 Political machinations

India is the world's largest democracy, with 340 million registered voters. Since Independence, the Congress Party (co-founded by Gandhi) have tended to hold power – though the right-wing, pro-Hindu BJP and its regional coalition partners have also formed governments in recent years.

Starting with Jawaharlal Nehru (India's first prime minister), the Nehru dynasty has dominated the Congress Party since 1947. After Indira Gandhi, Nehru's daughter, was assassinated in 1984, her son Rajiv took the reins until he too was murdered, in 1991. More recently, his Italian-born wife, Sonia, stepped up to lead Congress to a dramatic electoral victory in 2004, though she resigned immediately afterwards, stepping aside in favour of Dr Manmohan Singh.

"Do not blame God for having created the tiger, but thank him for not having given it wings."

Indian proverb

18 Record-breakers

- On July 26, 2005, Mumbai was deluged with 942mm/37.1 inches of rain – the most ever to fall on a city in a 24-hour period.
- Delhi tops the list of the world's most polluted cities, thanks to an explosion of private vehicle ownership over the past decade.
- Cherrapunji, in the northeastern hill state of Meghalaya, is officially the wettest place on earth. In one year (1860–61) it received 22,987mm (904.9 inches) of rain.
- The highest temperature recorded in India was 50.6 °C (123.1 °F) in Alwar in 1955. The lowest was -45 °C (-49 °F) in Kashmir.
- India's highest mountain, Nanda Devi (7821m/25,645ft), hasn't been climbed since 1982. The Indian government closed the peak to mountaineers after rumours got out that it had installed a nuclear-fuelled device on the summit to spy on neighbouring China.

 19 Festivals

▶▶ Most popular pilgrimages (of India's five main faiths)

- **Hinduism**: Kumbh Mela. Massive bathing ritual held in rotation on the banks of four sacred rivers. The 2001 Kumbh at Allahabad attracted 70 million worshippers. For more, see p.52.
- **Islam**: Urs Mela, Ajmer. Annual Saint's Day celebration (in Oct/Nov) at the tomb of revered Sufi mystic, Khwaja Muin-ud-din Chishti.
- **Jainism**: Mahamastakabhisheka Ceremony, Sravanabelgola. Vast quantities of milk, gold leaf and paints (including some from a helicopter) are poured over the colossus of Gomateshvara. Staged every 12 years, with the next scheduled for 2017.
- **Buddhism**: Mahabodhi Temple, Bodh Gaya. The site where the Buddha achieved enlightenment, visited in greatest numbers between November and February.
- **Christianity**: Exposition of Saint Francis Xavier's remains, Old Goa. Every ten years, Catholics from all over the world travel to Goa for a glimpse of the "Apostle of the Indies" supposedly incorruptible corpse. The next one's in 2014.

20 Language

Hindi, the mother tongue of 200 million natives of northern India, is the country's official language – but there are no fewer than 22 other nationally recognized languages, including Tamil, Malayalam, Gujarati, Punjabi, Bengali and Oriya. English is the lingua franca for business and, increasingly, education.

Known to have been spoken since the second millennium BC, Sanskrit is the subcontinent's ancient linguistic taproot. Today, its use is confined mainly to temples and sacred or historical texts.

▶▶ Ten English words derived from Hindustani

loot; pariah; dungarees; dinghy; khaki; shampoo; cushy; pyjamas; thugs; juggernauts

21 Natural disasters

▸▸ Five recent natural disasters

Sept 29, 1993	Latur earthquake, Maharashtra. 10,000–20,000 dead.
Oct 29, 1999	Supercyclone, Orissa. 10,000–20,000 dead.
2000	Drought in the northwest affects 32 million farmers; floods in the southeast displace 12 million.
Jan 26, 2001	Republic Day earthquake, Gujarat. Upwards of 30,000 killed.
Dec 26, 2004	Boxing Day tsunami. Offical estimates placed death toll at 11,000.

22 Plundered masterpieces

▸▸ Five priceless Indian art treasures in foreign museums

1. **The Amaravati Marbles**, British Museum, London. Dozens of elaborately sculpted railing friezes and panels from one of ancient India's most important Buddhist sites. c.200 BC to 200 AD.

2. **The Sanchi Torso**, Victoria & Albert Museum, London. Damaged but exquisite torso of male Buddhist deity, Avlokitesvara. c.900 AD.

3. **The Padshanama**, Royal Museum, Windsor Castle. Bound folio of brilliantly coloured illustrations commissioned by Mughal emperor, Shah Jehan. Only opened once every 50 years to protect its delicate pigments from light damage. Seventeenth century.

4. **The Spreading Trees Emerald**, Kuwait National Museum. The most extraordinary gem of its kind in the world, carved to resemble swaying palms. 1585.

5. **The Kohinoor Diamond**, Tower of London. The legendary "Mountain of Light", carried off from Delhi by Persian invader Nadir Shah in 1739, and now part of the British crown jewels.

23 Music

▶▶ Five must-have CDs

Hariprasad Chaurasia, *Hari-Krishna: In Praise of Janmashtami* (Navras). India's flute maestro at his most sublime.

Bismillah Khan, *Live in London* (Navras). Superb live set from India's virtuoso player of the double-reeded *shennai*.

Ravi Shankar, *Ravi Shankar & Ali Akbar Khan in Concert* (Apple). Inspired sarod and sitar duet by two living legends of Indian classical music.

Asha Bhosle, *The Rough Guide to Bollywood Legends: Asha Bhosle* (Rough Guides Music). Greatest hits from the most recorded artiste in history.

Lata Mangueshkar, *The Rough Guide to Bollywood Legends: Lata Mangueshkar* (Rough Guides Music). Retrospective from the "Nightingale of India", Asha Bhosle's elder sister, and the Queen of Bollywood playback singing.

24 Indian ingenuity

As well as putting other countries' discoveries and inventions (chillies, cinema, railways) to idiosyncratic uses, the subcontinent can claim to have originated sugar and cotton cultivation, the mathematical concept of zero, binary number systems, snooker and chess.

"We owe a lot to Indians, who taught us how to count – without which no scientific discovery could have been made."

Albert Einstein

 # **Women**

▶▶ **Five female high-flyers**

- **Rani Lakshmi Bhai** (1828–58). Queen of Jhansi state and heroine of the first War of Independence (aka the Indian Mutiny).

- **Indira Gandhi** (1917–84). Former Indian prime minister 1966–77 & 1980–84.

- **Jayalalitha** (1948–). Former movie starlet and Chief Minister of Tamil Nadu, notorious for her corruption and extravagant lifestyle.

- **Rani Mukerji** (1978–). Current Queen of Bollywood; the only woman to feature in Filmfare's "Ten Most Powerful Names in Bollywood".

- **Phoolan Devi** (1963–2001). Former dacoit, popularly known as the Bandit Queen, who later became a politician.

25

Ultimate

experiences

India

small print

ROUGH GUIDES – don't just travel

We hope you've been inspired by the experiences in this book. To us, they sum up what makes India such an extraordinary and stimulating place to travel. There are 24 other books in the 25 Ultimate Experiences series, each conceived to whet your appetite for travel and for everything the world has to offer. As well as covering the globe, the 25s series also includes books on **Journeys, World Food, Adventure Travel, Places to Stay, Ethical Travel, Wildlife Adventures** and **Wonders of the World**.

When you start planning your trip, Rough Guides' new-look guides, maps and phrasebooks are the ultimate companions. For 25 years we've been refining what makes a good guidebook and we now include more colour photos and more information – on average 50 percent more pages – than any of our competitors. Just look for the sky-blue spines.

Rough Guides don't just travel – we also believe in getting the most out of life without a passport. Since the publication of the bestselling Rough Guides to **The Internet** and **World Music**, we've brought out a wide range of lively and authoritative guides on everything from **Climate Change** to **Hip-Hop**, from **MySpace** to **Film Noir** and from **The Brain** to **The Rolling Stones**.

Publishing information

Rough Guide 25 Ultimate experiences India Published May 2007 by Rough Guides Ltd, 80 Strand, London WC2R 0RL
345 Hudson St, 4th Floor,
New York, NY 10014, USA
14 Local Shopping Centre, Panchsheel Park, New Delhi 110017, India
Distributed by the Penguin Group
Penguin Books Ltd,
80 Strand, London WC2R 0RL
Penguin Group (USA)
375 Hudson Street, NY 10014, USA
Penguin Group (Australia)
250 Camberwell Road, Camberwell, Victoria 3124, Australia
Penguin Books Canada Ltd,
10 Alcorn Avenue, Toronto, Ontario, Canada M4V 1E4
Penguin Group (NZ)
67 Apollo Drive, Mairangi Bay, Auckland 1310, New Zealand

Printed in China
© Rough Guides 2007
No part of this book may be reproduced in any form without permission from the publisher except for the quotation of brief passages in reviews.
80pp
A catalogue record for this book is available from the British Library
ISBN: 978-1-84353-812-7
The publishers and authors have done their best to ensure the accuracy and currency of all the information in Rough Guide 25 Ultimate experiences India; however, they can accept no responsibility for any loss, injury, or inconvenience sustained by any traveller as a result of information or advice contained in the guide.
1   3   5   7   9   8   6   4   2

Rough Guide credits

Author: David Abram
Editor: Edward Aves
Design & picture research: Diana Jarvis
Cartography: Katie Lloyd-Jones, Maxine Repath

Cover design: Diana Jarvis, Chloë Roberts
Production: Aimee Hampson, Katherine Owers
Proofreaders: Sarah Eno, Alison Murchie, David Paul

The author

Dave Abram writes Rough Guides to Goa, Kerala and Corsica, and is co-author of the Rough Guides to India and South India.

Picture credits

Cover Hindu woman bathing in the Ganges, Varanasi © Jens Storch/Alamy
2 Fresco, cave 17, Ajanta © Lindsay Hebberd/Corbis
6 Marigolds on sale, Mumbai © Sylvia Cordaiy Photo Library Ltd/Alamy
8–9 Ice waterfall, Zanskar © Oliver Föllmi/Hachette Photos

10–11 Thrissur Puram © southindiapicture/Hornbil Images Pvt Ltd/Alamy
12–13 On the set of Khamosh, Mumbai © Sherwin Crasto/Reuters/Corbis; movie posters © Mike Ford
14–15 Thali vegetarian meal © Simon Reddy/Alamy
16–17 Sadhus meditating at Gau Mukh © Nigel Hicks/Alamy

Fly Less – Stay Longer!

New Zealand

Budapest

Thailand

Greece

Punk

Italy

India

Over 70 reference books and hundreds of travel
guides, maps & phrasebooks that cover the world.

ROUGH GUIDES — Blogging

ROUGH GUIDES — Australia

ROUGH GUIDES — Cuba

ROUGH GUIDES — Britain

ROUGH GUIDES — Singapore

ROUGH GUIDES — Vietnam

ROUGH GUIDES — New York City

ROUGH GUIDES — Morocco

BROADEN YOUR HORIZONS
www.roughguides.com

ROUGH GUIDES 25 YEARS

Index